# THE BUSINESS OF BEING A STYLE INFLUENCER

BY ANITA NAHTA AMIN

CAPSTONE PRESS
a capstone imprint

Capstone Captivate is published by Capstone Press, an imprint of Capstone.
1710 Roe Crest Drive, North Mankato, Minnesota 56003
www.capstonepub.com

Copyright © 2021 by Capstone. All rights reserved. No part of this publication may be reproduced in whole or in part, or stored in a retrieval system, or transmitted in any form or by any means, electronic, mechanical, photocopying, recording, or otherwise, without written permission of the publisher.

**Library of Congress Cataloging-in-Publication Data**
Names: Amin, Anita Nahta, author.
Title: The business of being a style influencer / by Anita Nahta Amin.
Description: North Mankato, Minnesota : Capstone Press, [2021] | Series: Influencers and economics | Includes bibliographical references and index. | Audience: Ages 8–11 | Audience: Grades 4–6 | Summary: "Do you like trying new hair and makeup products? Are you always the first of your friend group to wear new trends? Then you might be on track to become a social media style influencer. Learn how your original takes on fashion could translate into a career by exploring the economics and business skills behind influencer marketing, while staying safe online." —Provided by publisher.
Identifiers: LCCN 2020034830 (print) | LCCN 2020034831 (ebook) | ISBN 9781496695710 (hardcover) | ISBN 9781977154996 (pdf) | ISBN 9781977156617 (kindle edition)
Subjects: LCSH: Fashion—Blogs—Juvenile literature. | Beauty, Personal—Blogs—Juvenile literature. | Fashion merchandising—Juvenile literature. | Cosmetics—Internet marketing—Juvenile literature. | Video blogs—Juvenile literature. | Product demonstrations—Juvenile literature. | Social influence—Juvenile literature. | Social media—Economic aspects—Juvenile literature.
Classification: LCC TT503.5 .A45 2021 (print) | LCC TT503.5 (ebook) | DDC 746.9/2—dc23
LC record available at https://lccn.loc.gov/2020034830
LC ebook record available at https://lccn.loc.gov/2020034831

**Image Credits**
iStockphoto: MesquitaFMS, 4, Viktoriia Hnatiuk, 10; Newscom: akg-images, 33, AXELLE/BAUER-GRIFFIN / MEGA, 9, bee_nfluencer, 41; Shutterstock: BONNINSTUDIO, 16, davooda, Cover (watch), Daxiao Productions, 6, Dean Drobot, 26, Diego Cervo, 30, GaudiLab, 13, 35, Gorodenkoff, 44, Hein Nouwens, Cover (fashion), Helen_st, 22, LightField Studios, 20, MikhalchukStudio, 27, Miro Vrlik Photography, 43, Monkey Business Images, 25, Motortion Films, 18, MPH Photos, 32, Rawpixel.com, 19, 24, 39, Reamolko, Cover (clothes), RedlineVector, Cover (dress), sheff, 36, tanuha2001, 15, Vasilisa Petruk, 40, Worawee Meepian, 29

**Editorial Credits**
Editor: Peter Mavrikis; Designer: Brann Garvey; Media Researcher: Morgan Walters; Production Specialist: Tori Abraham

All internet sites appearing in back matter were available and accurate when this book was sent to press.

Printed and bound in the USA. PO 3837

# CONTENTS

**SWAY WITH STYLE** .................... 5

CHAPTER 1
**WHAT IS A STYLE INFLUENCER?** ......... 6

CHAPTER 2
**GETTING STARTED** .................... 12

CHAPTER 3
**MAKING MONEY** ...................... 26

CHAPTER 4
**GROWING YOUR BUSINESS** ............. 38

TIMELINE ............................ 45
GLOSSARY ........................... 46
READ MORE .......................... 47
INTERNET SITES ...................... 47
INDEX ............................... 48

Words in **bold** are in the glossary.

# SWAY WITH STYLE

A million-dollar smile, a sleek outfit, and a hairstyle fit for a Hollywood star. You're ready for your photo shoot! The camera clicks. You try a hundred poses—silly, dreamy, mysterious. Finally, you catch the perfect one. Your fans will love what you're wearing. And if they like and share your photo on social media, you'll make thousands of dollars!

Now, it's time to pack up and go. You're flying first-class to Paris for a fashion show! You'll showcase sportswear for a brand-name company to your online fans. The clothes are so new that they won't be in stores for months. And the company has paid for everything, including your front-row seats.

Your fans are waiting to see what you wear next. Welcome to the world of a style influencer!

### CHAPTER 1
# WHAT IS A STYLE INFLUENCER?

*What should I wear? Do these socks match this outfit? How should I fix my hair?* Every day, thoughts like these cross countless minds. A style influencer can make it easier to choose the right look.

Style covers fashion and beauty topics. Fashion includes clothes, shoes, and accessories. Beauty focuses on makeup, hair, nails, and more.

# Persuasive Promoter

Style influencers share their views online about fashion, beauty, or both—all with the hope of swaying others to follow their lead. According to influencer marketing firm *MediaKix*, more than half of shoppers between the ages 8 to 24 would buy what an influencer likes over a movie star's choice. Influencers can be more persuasive than celebrities!

Influencers are often paid to promote products for brand companies. Young people spend more time online and less time watching television. TV commercials are no longer as widely viewed. One-fifth of users block internet ads, but one-third of internet time is spent on **social media**. So brand companies are relying more and more on influencers for online social media advertising to reach people instead.

## Fast Fact!

In ancient times, people thought influence was a magic power. In fact, influence is the ability to sway others and get them to think or act a certain way.

## Social Media Star

Influencers share their views online in social media **posts**. They often upload photos and videos. Many also have their own websites where they write blog articles. Some record podcast audio shows too.

A person can sign up online to follow an influencer on social media. This helps the follower keep track of new content. Followers and influencers span all ages. They may live across the world from each other. But social media connects them.

Child influencers are called *kidfluencers*—such as American fashion twins Ava and Leah Clements. They started modeling at age 7 in 2017. Now, they have almost 2 million Instagram followers! Sometimes, kidfluencers are babies or young children with social media accounts set up by their parents.

### America's First Supermodel
Before influencers, there were supermodels like Audrey Munson. Born in 1891 in New York, she is thought to be America's first supermodel. Many statues were made to look like her. After the Statue of Liberty, the next largest statue of a woman in New York City is of her!

Kidfluencers Ava and Leah Clements, also known as the Clements twins, have already worked with many brands, including Nike, Disney, Mattel, and Target.

## Moneymaker

Style influencers entertain fans on social media, but they may wear many other hats too. They model in fashion shows. They teach beauty lessons. They review products. They run businesses and pay bills, meet with clients, and work long hours. Some influencers even manage staff in an office.

Through many of these activities, influencers earn income. The fashion market is worth more than $1 trillion. Influencing is an $8 billion market and is expected to keep growing. Some influencers—including kids—make millions of dollars a year!

# Levels

There are different levels of influencers based on follower count. These levels may vary, depending on whom you ask. Someone is often considered a micro-influencer when they have 10,000 to 100,000 followers. But a macro-influencer, such as a celebrity, has more than 1 million. Most influencers on social media are micro-influencers. So if you're just starting out, you'll be in good company! You don't need a million followers to work as a style influencer.

## Influencer Levels

| Number of Followers | Influencer |
|---|---|
| < 10,000 | Nano |
| 10,000–100,000 | Micro |
| 100,000–1 Million | Mid-level |
| > 1 Million | Macro |

# CHAPTER 2
# GETTING STARTED

Style is a broad category that covers both fashion and beauty. So first, decide what to highlight.

Do you want to showcase complete makeup looks or whole outfit ensembles? Or would you rather narrow your scope? Some influencers focus on one area of style, such as purses or eye makeup. Others only work with certain color palettes, such as neutrals. Do you like pairing thrift store finds? What about sportswear, plus-size, or high-end fashion? Choose what inspires you so you can inspire others.

## Fast Fact!
Until the 1900s, pockets were not part of a girl's dress. They were separate and tied around a girl's waist with string, under her dress.

Planning and setting goals before you post will set up your business for success.

Starting out as a style influencer can be hard. Read agency blogs such as *MediaKix* to learn more about the market. Follow style influencers such as the Clements twins to better understand how they work. Pick your audience—the people you want to create content for. Will it be kids, teenagers, girls, boys? Different audiences may have different interests, and your interests should match theirs.

# Create Your Brand

Your brand is all about you—your attitude and what you want to be known for. Find a way to stand out from other influencers. If your content isn't unique, people won't need to follow you because they can find the same info elsewhere.

Influencers often have a website to showcase their brand and link all their social media accounts in one spot. To set up a website, ask an adult to help pick a **website host** and register your website address. Some hosts charge a fee of a few dollars per month. You can use the host's tools to create your website or pay a professional to build it for you.

Your website should include a biography to introduce yourself. You can add a **logo** too. A logo is a visual way to represent your brand. It helps people spot you among thousands of other influencers. You can make a logo using an online logo maker, many of which are free.

Recognize these fashion brand logos? Your logo should be simple but memorable too.

## Plan Your Workspace

Influencer photos often show scenic settings to add interest. Scout places such as a park or your yard. Make sure it's not too crowded or noisy if you'll be filming videos.

If you want a studio, a room at home might work. Check the space for good lighting or consider buying a light kit. In some cities, social media companies offer equipped studios if you meet a minimum follower count—often 10,000 or more.

Don't forget about all your equipment! You'll need a computer and internet connection for online tasks. To take photos and videos, you can use a smartphone or web cam, or buy a camera or camcorder. Some influencers use tripods to hold their cameras steady and microphones for better sound quality. You might need supplies and props—clothing, makeup, hair care products, and other materials. And when you're done taking photos, you can polish the pics with editing software. The cost of each piece of equipment ranges from free to hundreds of dollars.

## Equipment Needed

- Computer
- Internet connection
- Camera
- Video camera
- Photo editing software
- Props
- Clothes and/or makeup
- Light kit (optional)
- Tripod (optional)
- Microphone (optional)

# Plan Your Time

It can take hours to make props, film, and edit content for a 1-minute video. **Burnout** is a common problem among influencers. Taking breaks and pacing yourself are important. Scheduling content in advance can help. Many influencers make a monthly calendar to track what, where, and when they'll post.

Signs of burnout include feeling stressed, extremely tired, and uninterested in things you usually enjoy. If you feel this way, consider talking with a mental health professional.

Creating new content is important so followers don't get bored. Stay consistent too. Then your fans will know what to expect. For example, maybe your followers will look forward to beauty tips every Friday!

**Human capital** is measured as worker talent and labor time. Decide how much human capital to spend. Include everyone you work with. Do you need a professional photographer? Will friends model in a photo? Do you need to create sets? Everyone's time, including yours, has value—even if money isn't traded.

## Get Social!

The most common social media platforms for style influencers are Instagram, YouTube, and TikTok. Instagram allows photos, videos, and temporary slideshows. YouTube lets you post videos up to 12 hours long. TikTok is for videos shorter than 15 seconds. Children younger than 13 years old must get a parent or guardian's consent to open a YouTube or Instagram account. An adult must also help run the account. For TikTok, the age requirement is 16.

20

Influencers can get special social media accounts. These offer tools to study which posts interest followers. They also have ways to earn more income. Getting these accounts often requires a certain follower count.

Which social media platform should you choose? Keep in mind technology changes frequently. Platforms fade away to make room for new favorites. Features that influencers depend on for income could be removed. So it's a good idea to be active on multiple platforms.

## Social Media Platforms

**Instagram**
- Photos
- Videos up to 1 minute
- Instagram IGTV—videos ranging 1 minute to 1 hour, as well as series
- Instagram Stories—temporary slideshow of photos and videos

**YouTube**
- Videos up to 12 hours

**TikTok**
- Videos up to 15 seconds, but may put clips together for stories up to 60 seconds

## Stand Out From the Crowd

In a jumble of earrings, it's hard to find a specific one—unless the earring stands out somehow. The same is true for influencers. You have to make yourself visible to get noticed.

### Fast Fact!

More than 100 million photos and videos are posted on Instagram each day! And users tend to like blue in a photo more than red.

When users search online for content, influencers hope their posts show up at the top of the list. A formula drives where each post lands in the list of search results. The formula is based on your video quality and length, views and likes, how often you post, and more. But the formula changes often, making it hard to predict.

One way to make your post easier to find is by using a **hashtag**. Users on social media can filter posts by hashtag. This helps you reach people interested in your type of content.

## Popular Style Hashtags

- #fashion
- #style
- #beauty
- #hairstyle
- #ootd—outfit of the day
- #wiw—what I wore
- #styleinspo
- #makeupideas
- #wakeupandmakeup
- #selfie

## Build a Community

Now, it's time to hop online and start influencing! Be active, so people get to know you. Be authentic, so people grow to trust you. Ninety-three percent of followers will leave if they think you're insincere.

Some influencers cheat by buying fake followers from online companies. They hire **click farms** and **bots** to view and like posts. This type of fraud costs advertisers $1.3 billion a year. Many companies now study influencer posts to catch fakes.

Take time to build a following of real people who like and interact with your posts. It'll pay off!

Bullying online is called cyberbullying, and it's never OK. Speak with a trusted adult if you feel unsafe.

## Staying Safe

Influencers connect with people every day, and sometimes they may face bullies and stalkers. Decide ahead of time how to handle them with a parent or guardian. Decide how much of your life story to share. Remember to never share your location online.

Bullying is against the rules and can result in account shutdown. Some social media platforms have built-in tools to block or report bullies. Remember that the rules apply to you too. Don't make negative comments about other people or businesses online. You might hurt someone's feelings, lose followers, or even get in serious trouble!

**CHAPTER 3**

# MAKING MONEY

*Cha-ching!* Are you ready for the cash to roll in? It might take a few months—or years—but don't get discouraged! Many influencers started in the same shoes as you.

Brands will often send influencers products, such as makeup, to try for free in the hopes the influencer will post about it.

There are lots of ways to earn money as an influencer. Followers may pay to subscribe to your channel or access exclusive content. Viewers can choose to donate money. Some platforms such as YouTube pay influencers each time they attach an ad to their videos. Instagram and TikTok are also making plans to share ad revenue.

Sometimes instead of money, influencers get freebies such as makeup, luxury trips, event tickets, pedicures, education, and more. Many influencers also create their own beauty or fashion lines to sell to fans. For example, the Clements twins launched their own line of socks and slippers.

## Shop Till You Drop

If a person buys a product you recommend, you can earn money! Platforms either have or are testing the ability to click a link and shop for a product shown in an influencer post. The influencer gets a cut of the income if the viewer buys the product. Third-party companies offer revenue share deals too. Some of these companies, such as RewardStyle, are by invitation only, but they offer a broader shopping experience with the potential to earn even more.

### Closet Accounts

Fans often want to wear what an influencer wears. But the fans may not know where to find the outfit. A closet account tracks a star's latest trends. Teens often run this type of account on Instagram for fun, not to earn money. They race to be the first to break the news on what a star wears, where to find it, and how much it costs.

Many influencers open online shops through **e-tailers** to sell their own designs or other brands. Influencers also sell secondhand clothes through thrift shops or online resale programs. But they often pay a commission on sales—as high as 20 percent! This cuts into their **profit**. Instead, some influencers take pictures of their closets and share new items for sale on Instagram each week. Many sell out in a few hours!

Amazon is one of the world's most popular e-tailers. Online stores can offer an easy way for fans to shop influencer merchandise.

29

## Become a Brand Ambassador

Brand companies hire influencers to advertise their products online in posts. If you don't have thousands of followers, don't worry! Brands are working more and more with micro- and nano-influencers. These influencers tend to have closer bonds with their followers. The followers are often more engaged. So the brand's profit is higher compared to spending a lot to hire very famous influencers.

When you work with a brand, tell a story about how its products help you. But remember to stay authentic. Choose only brands that match your own brand. Think about if your audience will want to hear about them and their products.

To connect with brands, find an **agent**, join a social media program such as TikTok's creator marketplace, or join an e-tailer. Brands will often seek out influencers too. They'll look at an influencer's content and style. They'll also check follower count and engagement. Engagement is based on how many times a follower shares, likes, clicks, or comments on posts.

## Fast Fact!

Bosses at TikTok are required to make and upload films. If their videos don't get a certain number of likes, the owner makes them do push-ups!

FTC rules about paid posts protect consumers against dishonest business practices. This helps people of all ages make better decisions when buying products.

## Follow the Rules

If you're paid to post content, the **Federal Trade Commission** (FTC) requires you by law to tell your followers. Young children watching your channel may not understand what a commercial is or that you're in one. They may think you're trying something for fun.

Influencers must add a label such as a hashtag like #Ad or #Sponsored at the beginning of a post or in a noticeable spot. You must tell followers even if the product was free. And you can't promote a product you didn't use or like.

Another law influencers need to know is the Children's Online Privacy Protection Act (COPPA). It bans websites from collecting data from children. In response, YouTube will ban certain ads. They will also turn off comments on kids' sites and bury the sites in searches. This may decrease influencer earnings.

Each state has its own child labor laws. Some states want to apply these laws to online influencer jobs. This includes requiring Coogan Accounts, which protect child income.

## The Coogan Act

Child star Jackie Coogan lost his fortune to greedy adults. The Coogan Act shields child actors' wages. Fifteen percent of their income must be put into special bank accounts called Coogan Accounts until age 18. So far, California and a few other states have this law or a law like it. It doesn't include child influencers. But lawmakers want to change this.

Jackie Coogan was popular in silent films of the 1920s.

# Pay Day!

How much are influencers paid for making posts about brands? There are a few ways to decide pay rates. Typically, Instagram posts fetch $10 or more per 1,000 followers. For fashion and beauty, though, the rate can go up to $1 or more for every follower!

Some brands pay an hourly rate instead and reimburse the influencer for money spent making the commercial. Other brands pay based on how engaged the influencer's followers are. But engagement can't measure how many people talk about the product offline. So don't be afraid to **negotiate**!

## Fast Fact!
Earning money is the most common reason people become influencers. Another top reason is to help others.

> Confidence is key to negotiating. Be polite but firm. Know the value of your services and know when to walk away.

To persuade the brand to raise your fee, you could offer to throw in freebies. That might be something such as additional photos. If the brand won't let you work with anyone else at the same time, you could also negotiate a higher fee because of lost income with other brands.

# Don't Break Your Budget

It's exciting to make money as an influencer. But you'll probably also have to spend money to get your business going.

If you make more than what you spend each year, congratulations! Your business is gaining money. This is called a profit. If you spend more than what you make, your business is losing money. This is called a loss. The difference between earnings and cost is the total profit or loss. The goal is to make a profit by earning more or spending less than what you earn.

A budget can help you stay on track. First, list your income. This could include money earned from revenue share deals, paid posts, and more.

Next decide how much to save. You won't use this money for everyday spending. If you put your savings in a bank, the money grows with **interest**. For example, you save $5,000 in a bank and it pays 5 percent interest a year. After five years, you'll have $6,381. The bank paid you $1,381 for storing your money with them!

Finally, list each upcoming expense, including equipment. Taxes are also an expense. Each year, you must pay a part of your income to the U.S. government. Taxes must also be paid on any product received for free as part of your influencer work.

### Fast Fact!

Early banks lent seeds, not coins. Farmers would grow crops for food and pay back loans with new seeds.

# CHAPTER 4
# GROWING YOUR BUSINESS

When you string beads together, you don't put all of them on at once. You slide each bead down the string, one by one, taking care not to let the others slip off and roll away. Growing your business is similar. Followers will join little by little. Each new follower adds to your future income potential.

Word of mouth is one of your greatest sources for growth. People tend to follow the herd—if it looks good to some people, others think it must be good too. Find out what makes your followers happy by studying which posts got more views, likes, and clicks. Add more of that type of content.

## Fast Fact!

Jewelry made of hair was common in the 1800s. People used the hair of loved ones to make keepsake rings and more. They wove their own hair as gifts too.

Happy viewers are often engaged viewers, which can lead to more opportunities to earn money.

# Stay in the Game . . . and Win!

The supply of influencers keeps growing. Eighty-six percent of young people want to be one! But what happens if everyone tries to become an influencer? The market will overload and become too full. Then it will be hard for influencers to find work. Brands will be able to choose whomever they want. Influencers will have to compete against each other.

To stay ahead of the competition, you must offer unique content. This way, the demand for your services will stay high. Building relationships with brands and followers will help keep their loyalty in a down market too.

Keep your content special and fresh so everyone will want to hear your fashion takes!

Your competition won't just come from humans. Artificial intelligence is a player in the market. Some computer generated images (CGIs) look so real, many people think they're actual humans. CGI character "Lil Miquela" has 2.3 million Instagram followers and models for famous brands. While humans make mistakes, CGIs are easier to control. Artificial intelligence has also been used to put together personalized outfits for customers. Most customers liked these outfits more than those picked by influencers.

CGIs don't have to be human. B is a CGI bee that appears in social media posts to raise awareness about environmental issues.

## Fast Fact!

Lil Miquela is said to be the first CGI influencer. She started on Instagram in April 2016.

## Step into the Spotlight

Show off your brand! Let people know you're out there and that you're serious about your business. Promote your sites through other influencers, bloggers, and brands, especially if they're established. Their followers may follow you and mention you to others.

Many influencers are active outside of social media too. They may design their own fashion or beauty lines—such as kidfluencer Millie-Belle Diamond, who launched her own baby clothing line. They also model during Fashion Week in New York, Milan, London, or Paris. Kidfluencer Taylen Biggs walked the New York fashion runway when she was just 3 years old! They even appear in movies and on television, such as influencer Chiara Ferragni who was a judge on a fashion reality TV series. Influencing can open new doors if you engage with others.

a New York Fashion Week runway show in February 2015

## New York Fashion Week

New York Fashion Week started in 1943 and is held twice a year. It has hundreds of fashion shows where models strut down the catwalk in designer clothes. Front-row seats were once saved for fashion magazine editors and celebrities. Now, influencers sit there too! They model clothes for brands there and post about it online.

## A Stylish Future

Fashion and beauty are among the highest paying influencer markets. It's not all glamour all the time, though. The hours can be grueling—a whirlwind of photo sessions, brand events, social media communication, and more. There are many influencer hopefuls. Not everyone succeeds. But patience, respect for your audience, unique content, and hard work can help you shine like a jewel!

# Timeline

**1940**
- 1943 – First New York Fashion Week

**1950**
- 1960s – U.S. military invents ARPANET, a network that allows distant computers to transfer information.

**1960**

**1970**
- 1983 – ARPANET opens to the public as internet.

**1980**
- 2005 – First YouTube video posted
- 2009 – Chiara Ferragni starts The Blonde Salad fashion blog.

**1990**
- 2010 – Instagram starts.

**2000**
- 2013 – Beauty influencer Huda Kattan launches her own beauty brand.

**2010**
- 2016 – TikTok is formed.

**2020**
- 2016 – Lil Miquela appears on Instagram.

45

# GLOSSARY

**agent** (AY-juhnt)—a person hired to make business deals for someone else

**bot** (BOT)—a computer program that can run on its own

**burnout** (BURN-out)—a state of being very physically and emotionally tired from working too much

**click farm** (KLIK FAHRM)—a company that adds fake views to posts

**e-tailer** (EE-tay-luhr)—an online shop

**Federal Trade Commission** (FED-er-uhl TREYD kuh-MISH-uhn)—the U.S. government agency that makes sure businesses follow the law; abbreviated FTC

**hashtag** (HASH-tag)—a tag to group online posts and aid in searches; starts with #

**human capital** (HYOO-muhn KAH-puh-tuhl)—the value of a worker's skills toward meeting a goal

**interest** (IN-ter-ist)—a charge a borrower pays a lender

**logo** (LOH-goh)—a symbol meant to stand for a company

**negotiate** (ni-GOH-shee-ate)—to discuss something in order to come to an agreement

**post** (POHST)—something shared online, such as photos or a video

**profit** (PRAH-fit)—money earned after expenses are paid

**social media** (SOH-shuhl MEE-dee-uh)—websites people use to share content

**website host** (WEB-sahyt HOHST)—a service which has computers to keep and run websites

# READ MORE

Berne, Emma Carlson. *Understanding Advertising*. North Mankato, MN: Capstone Press, 2019.

Dell, Pamela. *Understanding Social Media*. North Mankato, MN: Capstone Press, 2019.

Ruscik, Jessica. *JoJo Siwa*. Minneapolis: ABDO Publishing, 2020.

# INTERNET SITES

*The Mint*
themint.org/kids/

*New York Public Library Internet Safety Tips*
nypl.org/help/about-nypl/legal-notices/internet-safety-tips/

*Pacer Center's Kids Against Bullying*
pacerkidsagainstbullying.org/

# INDEX

ads and advertising, 7, 27, 30, 32, 33
agents, 31
artificial intelligence, 41
audiences, 13, 31, 44

brands, 29, 40, 41, 43, 44
   working with, 7, 30–31, 34–35
budgeting, 36–37
burnout, 18

click farms, 24
closet accounts, 28
computer generated images (CGIs), 41
Coogan Accounts, 33
cyberbullying, 25

engagement, 30, 31, 34, 42
equipment, 17, 37
e-tailers, 29, 31

Federal Trade Commission (FTC), 32
freebies, 27, 32, 35, 37

hashtags, 23, 32
human capital, 19

income, 10, 21, 28, 33, 35, 37, 38
influencer branding, 14, 31, 42
influencer levels, 11, 30
Instagram, 8, 20, 21, 22, 27, 28, 29, 34, 41, 45

kidfluencers, 8, 10, 33, 42
   Clements twins, 8, 13, 27

laws, 32, 33
logos, 14

modeling, 8, 10, 19, 41, 42, 43
   Munson, Audrey, 8

negotiating, 34, 35
New York Fashion Week, 42, 43, 45

online safety, 25

pay rates, 34, 44
posts, 8, 21, 23, 24, 28, 30, 31, 32, 34, 37, 38
profits, 29, 30, 36

revenue sharing, 28, 37

schedules, 18
selling products, 27, 29
social media, 7, 8, 10, 11, 14, 16, 23, 31, 42, 44
   platforms, 20–21, 25
subscriptions, 27

taxes, 37
TikTok, 20, 21, 27, 31, 45
tools, 14, 21, 25

websites, 8, 14, 33, 42

YouTube, 20, 21, 27, 33, 45